www.finishinglinepress.com

The Gate of Play

poems by

Joseph Hamel

Finishing Line Press
Georgetown, Kentucky

The Gate of Play

Publisher: Leah Maines

Editor: Christen Kincaid

Cover Art: Joseph Hamel

Author Photo: Nicholas Martin-Smith

Cover Design: Elizabeth Maines McCleavy

Order online: www.finishinglinepress.com
also available on amazon.com

Author inquiries and mail orders:
Finishing Line Press
P. O. Box 1626
Georgetown, Kentucky 40324
U. S. A.

Table of Contents

friends teachers family

Once we kiss we will destroy

the Alone ourselves alone

Once we try to walk together
we will limp and

Once we start
the pain will travel

Everywhere

But we will try again.

A String

The fragile shaft of breath
without your having
discovered the source.

Enjoy the rhythms that yet return
and fill our senses

The warm blood
a string, a trickle.

We remember some pole, self, totem, icon

      and try to say
what we see
and fail

What do we hear or see?

Our mouths

Our eyes

We love the blue river
below the falling dark.

The stars and thunder

The splitting energy
of our bodies flexed as breath
in our embrace.

It shall pass

We have joined in the warm blood beat
of hiss, and labor, sleeping, murmurs.

It shall pass, asleep in each other

The voice of the one we become
in the kicking pleasure.

What has been shed and caressed and
eased from us sinks to the past evening.

Families, our births are in another world
disappearing into a hole of having to leave
and wanting to shed and wanting to grow.

The world of our cells of days and nights
is the life we tell ourselves to ourselves
about ourselves, our favorite story.

The voice of the male tied
together with the female.

Alone alone alone

You have escaped to a dead new life

You have upped and chucked it all

You have spurned the relationships
and reach for them and believe
you are new and dead and alive

As if feel you touch the loss of fear of life and death

And the new strangers will want your information
as did the old strangers

And you must allow them to misinterpret you
as did the original strangers
and as you misinterpreted them

And the new strangers will watch you walk alone and sit in the sun
and smile or not
and wonder

Why does he walk alone?

And you are wondering and
asking yourself

Who in fact do you think you are
sitting in the sun, smiling or not?

Who the hell do you think you are
with your mental so-called health
of being entirely by yourself and
this stream of freedom you feel
you flash around you like a tail or cape
to live anew, and feel the death
of all those beautiful years
and tools and plans

that live inside you and

Who in fact are you?

Smiling, wandering
beginning, ending and
waiting, looking and

What is this new
freedom and
the answer is nothing
but alone, alone, alone
but say

It is
heaven
to have left
but you suffer
a certain number of hell
days for it

It is your burden
but now and then you are released
to smile again

And it is not so new after all
and still it is sheer, the hunger and silence

And the mind racing
with the new unknown life on the street
and in standing in line alone briefly and
in boarding or disembarking and
this new existence, unsettled, unknown is a little sharp and
it's a little more than you want to impose on just anyone

So stay friendly but distant at first
to the new strangers as to the old

for your story remains
just a story, elsewhere

And all this is, is nothing new
and always has been common
and rare

And you feel sharp and blurred
and dead and alive to the past
and at the same time
solid and spirit, sitting on a hill

or walking through town and
all of it part of a cycle
in which you are caught
and which you freely joined
amounting to some meager
thoughts amounting to

Once again looking for home
and you can hardly bear
repeating such phrases as

My name is….

I come from…

I went to….

Because it starts to bore you

But you will be pleased
and unconcerned with
your new role
Because you feel a
greater risk
and chance to feel.

But alive and well
you are just a cell
and all you did
was divide
to become
the same
self, but with a sense
of something sharper
but, not always clear.

And then it is simpler
and you are just a cell

and the same old cell
and mother's son
as when you dreamed
of love and meaning.

You can feel that they are just there

love and meaning

waiting

staring at you

on the path

or at the window
of some building.

Decorating the past

It comes but you push it away

You advance towards the final ground of
settling down, your face splits and warps

You are the Self, pole, winner and failure
and figure who stuck where you stood
and where your work was arrayed
to be gathered by someone or parceled
and dispersed

All of it
had fit in a narrow corridor
of effort and survival

From the earliest fires, the mysterious, calm
and violent world, the nights and stars

To decorate the empty invisible future with
the language and art and fears we carved

One line or word, one note, a string or tongue
could stir so much of action, thought, belief.

It comes but you push it away.
That work and love are nearly done.

New world

Ourselves
the individual replicas, figures of lovers
and partners, smiled as we rode along
the settled river wilderness, into the land
at high speed and lay down to sleep at night

The mind's light scratching restlessly, dreaming

Nowhere was home or the promise of it

For years, we did not discover a fire
or a cottage in a wood

Ourselves
of clay and replicas like wax and symbols
representing something being effaced, eroding

If only all that water falling
could beautify pride and fear

If only the hum of the beating of bees in the field
busily, greedily in the vicinity of such astonishing
abundance of water, meant, we who should have
slept content at the great wonder of the world and
who churned our labor to coin so that we could trade
in trinkets and fuel and romance, could have arrived
in a home, and found in each other what we hoped

The guide repeats
in our memory
such words as

totem
pole
iron
ore

A voice in the spray on the ferry

and underneath the waterfall

But always on the tip of our tongue
was an animal thought of hunger
and flesh and yet a freeze like
black ice became our thoughts.

I finger the hard problem

I keep rubbing this stone of friendship
in a dream in which I am trying to say
everything I've been unable to say

I eat my words over and over

I am becoming a skin of wind
I am becoming a soul of bother

And then the stone
upon which my fingerprints wither

One day it will be used to close my mouth
as I disappear from the face of the earth

A last smile will secrete and trickle and
stretch the corner of my mouth

A last crack upon the mask I was
whoever I was

Enemy, friend
the love of someone
a stone in someone's hand.

Morning song

We step out of our room today
and feel innocent on a journey

That as long as we move
there is more to begin

We carry life and death
like a child in our arms

We carry a while and
then we walk along

It isn't that we cannot bear
the burdens of our arms
or that we need to know
what each embrace can mean

We bear the burden and we work and dream and
for a moment when we wake, before the day is truly lit

We may seek or glimpse and feel that we have time
to start again, something new. Or else we dream of solitude

A picture of a village in a warm country
or a wish for an ocean of ceaseless calm

Or to be able to disappear into a wood, like the fox
we saw slipping into trees, looking back at us as if
it was sick of being seen, tired of being followed
with its extinction ticking. That freedom we loved.

Time has torn apart its coat since then

Time has strangled its movement
and yet it remains as it had lived

It never craved the gift of afterlife

It never mattered, all its deaths
and wasn't guilty, innocent

It never formed a death wish
or could name a punishment.

Dawn clears the room

Dawn clears the room

We lie down for a second sleep

I feel my hands strangely paper clean
and dry against the sheets and yet

I close my eyes and see a spray
of water and a flooded ground
of sand and stone and tile and mud

I close my eyes and keep the scene
of yesterday before me:

You, bending over
under fountain water

Tiny waves
on concrete
by the drain
containing
insects

They start to move theirs wings
on the pavement in the water and
you step to avoid them

Your hair drips
and you leave the fountain
and walk on grass
and avoid the bees on clover

And back to the ocean
I follow you
across the sand
and over a rise of sand the wide water
and sky appears and the whole day

appears

And my eyes follow
you

And the eyes of anyone
watch your large shirt
over your breasts
over your hips.

This morning a
second sleep

Free of weight
free of loss

I stretch my hand but change my mind
and do not pass my palm too near your belly.

Closing my eyes
again

Only allowing
a little pressure
of reality
into dreaming
yesterday

Not even a story
and barely a dream
of yesterday

Forming
nothing

Lying still
in bed

dozing

Free of pain
free of blood
free of loss.

Your birthday likes to pedal round the year

Your birthday likes to pedal round the year
and bump into your arm and glass. Smile,
a little wine trickles on your hand, and
you lick it off.

Your birthday drips from leaves.
I want to love the yard and
the evening lying upon it
and come tangled to bed
in each other.

It is only another day.
Your birthday.

Certain foods
a memory
of respect
a kind of death.

It is only another day
we share, the sunny
glass globe of the air and blue
and hot light and yellow dryness
of the sound of the humming city
no matter where we are.

We are not yet done
changing the world.

We charm the coiled serpent Time
as we embrace.

Even as the sameness
is waiting for us outside.

Each day beyond the green picture
of darkness in the deepening streets

and dusk crushed into trees.

We do not have to be done
changing the world rolling the earth
between us
playing.

It is true
the sameness is waiting for us
outside.

Even for the most
beautiful moments
one cannot stay.

We live how we can

Raise the dress

and run away.

Once we kiss we will destroy
the Alone ourselves alone

Once we try to walk together
we will limp and

Once we start
the pain will travel

Everywhere

But we will try again.

**

Lie down in the middle of the night

The night has entered winter

Leaves are still on some trees

The river splits in long cracked sound holes
around the islands, white ice and dark water

The white panels of ice beneath
the white cloud sky
with slits open to the deep
blue of north wind and star light.

**

The blazing light of the city above
is set back away from the bluff

The river lies below where the moonlight

splinters in the dark trees along the bank.

**

Raise your dress and run away
as if in show, as if in fun

The open wildness

And the house is filled with white light
and red stains of dawn
against your back.

From day to night
and around and ever

The house is filled
with the sense of slow growth
of all we may accomplish.

**

I enter a room like a river opening wider, black and
with deepening groove of the known and unknown

Stiff bush touches my cheek when ducking my head deeper

The tips and stems of loose vegetation, caked and matted
scrape against my face, and further and further
I move under the broken water of grinding waves.

**

What was a name for
this ancient red river

How can I say

I am at peace
when you walk me home
when I lie against your blue fire
your dress

your eyes
your stars

your black loss
your kiss.

**

This meteoric slither, your twisting
rivulet our bones tied together
we journey and float

We knit the self
we spin
the current oneness
and convey
the river
from bottom to surface, within the silent part
of the body of taut power and soft walls
of water and pressure, disturbed and blown
into shaking, erupting and flooding
to layer the darkness around us.

A frozen thought in burning dust.

Creation springs at your banks of

Yourself
solitary
beating in the

life you breathe.

**

Where are we when we
climb away from the sunken position within the reeds

and can watch the river spread in bounty and survival

From where we stand together and lie together
we see creation.

What are we when we tie our bones together
and bleed the liquid

We are light like
nerves like stars
the cold world of
motionless space
the bottom of sleep

We live how we can
and suffer what we are given.

**

Undrape
your black shadows

Could you be blacker or whiter than the pure
potion of mystery scent that rises, peacefully
out of your body and mouth, clarity of gladness
and wonder at holding each other

**

Wait

if I undo the buttons this muscle moves

Wait

your hand has the strings of a nest
cupping your pulse

Cupped to raise a silent word
cupped with wind and water
and the strings of your wrist stream in the darkness

The blood flows the water enters and
they wind out of the center into the center

Wait

Our hips swim in the deep
by night and wake in the morning
to the winter bowl of the warm kiss.

**

The strings of your arms bind your shoulder
the strings of your neck display the breadth
of shivering power from the world your heart
beneath your breast

How can we be blacker and clearer and whiter
than stars and space when draped and undraped

Wait

A table and pillar
The column and path
of the darkness and sweat

The surface of your back and grounded

clasp of your opening and receiving

Your face self-known
unknown infinite

The eyes tense and glitter, tense
and flicker the white and black
comfort of pressure

The strings of your ridge below
the surface
the soft totem of gorging warmth

The soft totem moves and resists
far below the light and time

The creation of stars
by splitting a star.

**

Thinking

Mystery

The open wildness and strip of human contact

The years of growth and letting alone to flower

The field streamed blue and liquid with reactions to light

The piles of white covering the rounded gently rolling earth

The snow pink where the leaking red dawn stains the banks
and the river opening wider and free of ice looking full
and black and deepening the imagination to dream
of the further and further groove of the body of water

And the self, core and carved faces

The self, poles breathing ignorance

Your mouth opens facing death in bearing life

Returning from death with life your thighs the banks
the water's edge the motionless channel the orchard
and the thaw ooze running under the broken thin ice
at the edge of this path of halting peace wanting
to express the bottom of the self to anyone

To push away from a confusion and death

Your skin, your belly, billows, a sail
that we will push into the new world.

**

Where are we?

The call is on the tip of our tongues.

It is an animal thought you keep and release

An animal thought of our clear eyes and memories
flooding space with images overturning each other

Where are you?

You feel a ghost trying
to come free in spring
You feel partly of the earth
isolated, and a new

Cool emptiness of purpose
untouched, again

A vessel
a new meaning
and impermanence.

That is where we arrived

**

The simplest utterance
we offer each other

The voices we will push across a path
and push through time

**

Hold your hand out
steady
hold of relaxed
Passion.

Look where we began

Raise your dress

and run away

and I will follow

room to room

around the yard
and fields
and dawn.

Journey as I journey.

Let the memories flood and drown and forget

We will feel touched and untouched
a vessel, a ghost.

We have nothing in our hands.
No one knows who we are as we smile.

We who love and offer each other
Impermanence, Harmony.

The ocean would come to me

in the alone
sweet

Fester of alone passion
uncaring of high noon

Sweat-lick of the warm salt
drip of sweat
that rainbows
on a sprig of eyelashes

Blinking it down
to the mouth
and tongue

Blue sky
Ribbon above me
in the Crater of alone

Sitting on my heels
studying dirt
in a pool of hands

Barefooted
Gingerly
Stepping

Around the weeds
with needles

In the ocean of heat
and concrete
asphalt

A child grows
into the past

Expecting a future

The future grows smaller

and smaller
in time

The sky
stares blameless
and blue

A ribbon
of indifference

But
the child can't help
but love the
ocean of time
alone.

Death has always been your companion

in the family and living alone
as you steered loneliness

Death rests within you
as a bed below a river
and is the river itself

And stirred one day
you are carried away
and you are the river
and catch all of perceptions
and the elements

And one last look one day and one last
sense of the effort and labor, you were, of
love and pleasure, then all of it begins to drift

The man or woman you were
who looked into the world
drifts off, away

You will remember
all that effort to drive as far you could
and to touch the sweetest, deepest parts
of nature left, further and further, looking, hoping

And what of the losses of the forests battered
or all of the conflicts of the city or the world
and blowing of holes into sky and the earth
and all the needs and improvements to come?

You lived with all that effort, and you lived on it
as well and you stood out of its way and were
a part of it

But drifting off like bark and smoke you see
your life of having to negotiate desire and operate

your will, and how simply used up they are at last
and how they couldn't be kept and you never

possessed them

They were never yours, and you
dabbled with them briefly

The fallen figure

Totem and fossil
Doer
Thinker
in the world

Disintegrating
expressive
face of mystery.

Open the gate of play, an earliest memory

Open the gate of play, an earliest memory

immersion, of clear taste of air, water
and salt.
                    The boy and girl pull in secret

The water and sand yields. They have blacks
and whites hidden about them, mysteries

They each possess and sense, and play free
of who they are, and who are they?

                    Red hairs laced with brown
and blond and pale and tan; we have so much
calm, gray
and sweet blue and the shadows of mud and garage
and bush and the pink which appears delicious, inviting.

          Opening the gate of play.

Finger go down in mud.

The pull
of earth

The hidden clay, the looks in our eyes
and the length and limitations of gestures

Busily free of the world and the world moved
by our power and the world remaining fixed
in our moving the earth away
and our fascination as the water returns
again.

                    All this opening motion, and distortion.
Pushing a muscle and bone away, they return
the same;

opening sand and pressing away
the sea and sand return

and flood the hand
and weigh the arms.

           Sleep with me in memory
for the day has ended; live with me now in
darkness of an early memory;

lie together
in one of the earliest shadows
opening a gate of play.

The black green lip of water
below the golden strand of sand.

The pink smiles

The eyes and hair
dangle
in light.

When I saw Jane again she appeared

When I saw Jane again she appeared
with every atom of her being to be
in love
lying there, with him.

But I knew this like I knew trees

as a child thinks silently
and actively knowing
how it is
all at once

Beauty became her unmade love made face

Parents
are so afraid of death
carrying off everything.

At the far end of a playfield, down by the teeth
of the bottom of fence, within a stand of trees

Parents and priests burned in her fire
and shriveled to the back of her mind.

Snow white light in moonlight

Snow white light in moonlight
is the color of your skin

In the deep photograph profile carving
of black and white, a loose strand
of long hair along your cheek.

While driving on the interstate

Staring at the choker line
of pink and red sunset
on the horizon
and with eyes battered with
snowflakes in headlights
as night falls

Your voice passes through
the middle of wilderness as
the world falls into the black
region of highway and
the pitch black woods
following beside me

And the carving of black
and white photograph
remains.

Later inside my room
beauty comes for me.

Memory is fiction.

You curl into my embrace.
We pound the air in silence
spilling the sound of your voice.

We gather and scatter the real and unreal

We gather and scatter the real and unreal

And when we are on the black canal of return

Our hands become the first frost in deep sleep

And cold, the year winds up in a clean print
of our curious hands plunging in wet snow

But looking back

4 o'clock had ended the summer and
rang the first alarm of autumn

And all afternoon, and before noon
the light on the luxury of us gathering
our legs and arms and mouths together
in our spring and beginning in first light and

We gathered and scattered the real and unreal
all day, and plundered and shared and embraced
for years in a day, many years of a version of dust

And now on the black canal of return of dawn

The sun beats through the darkness to us
and our bodies like the day, shall begin again
and we'll hold each other's welcome patient love.

Out of the shadows

Boys and girls come out of the shadows
and sit inside us like ghosts or negatives

innocent deaths

of our childhoods

first encounters of love
of a man and a woman

A man and woman find peace and
myths, possibilities and monsters

Craving, meets craving

We kiss and the days and nights to come
fly around our heads
they fly to us

And for a moment or minutes we
joy to feel again the ancient love

The sea
older than animals

Older than bones
is sliding down
the columns
of our spines

We touch and feel that fluid, stir, and feel
we have words, and sometimes the will to use them
honestly.

In a shell of August heat

Sitting in a doorway, the open cell
of the driveway, against the brick wall

A side door slamming and the hollow bang
and metal pail sound of a milk chute, somewhere

In a shell of August heat with the flies
we shot with rubber bands

To feed the twitching wounded to
spiders' webs

All along those streets and lawn and driveways
the young men like sheaves
of limbs and growing beards
in loafers and sneakers

And the older girls:

I was level with their mystery
when gathered to their hips

And I stood as a kid at the big thighs
and I stood to Nancy's wish to dance
with her big hair, eyelashes
and happy, grand exuberance
of her generous mind.

We have always needed
an after-life, and here it is:
Memory.

Walls, schools and a life
we find where we can place
ourselves in afternoons
in living rooms once again

and Nancy, in the light of my formative years
in her first and lonely moments of boys.

Children and husband would come to tap her

and she was earth, fertility, joy
on a river of white carnations
in the litter of fake royal treatment.

The queen of a float of romance.

Her parade of affectionate fire.

She would bear the badges
and rings and desire.

I watch her depart the school auditorium
with her freedom, her sweetness, prospects
of kitchen, collapse, college, and children
and her Czarina smile of death and peace.

A pom-pom-ed, veiled, and pleated package
of blossoms, among men and children.

I love her kindness, her face.

You turn into a brief of phrases

At the behest of the three or four
needs, 5 or 7 appointments of life
and death

You must remain the soul of politeness.

*

In the history of houses

There came one fire to return to.
There was s door that made a difference.

*

The home packs us into the world and we dream
progress, history, archive, journey, and humanity

*

All you want is the time to learn one thing
out of all the noise that rises over the walls
each day.

*

Outside, the endless debt for some, the danger of sunset.

The hope of children, how new they may dream
as beings apart from us, at first.

The spring in their pursuit.

The threats to their minds and bodies.

*

The highway registers the open wildness
and straight rule of contact that is work.

You shall warp over time but keep it up

And then you quit, move on. A path opens.

*

For a time it made sense to appoint, design

as when you said this root goes there
and that thought remains fixed

And as a frame of reference
this is when we eat

*

As far as the government is concerned
some actions are attempted to make this come out right.

*

In the history of a life it's on you.

How to use the breath
in your body

The right to say
what goes
what gives

*

Every day and three times a day

we go outside and come back home

and come through the door feeling
definite as a key and follow each other
around or we shoot through the rooms

And there is love on the bedrock
of love, and duty, trying to
soothe the hot pain of living
and how much we are unloved
or not liked or superficially regarded
and disdained with politely
callous careless rejections

*

Orbiting never tires the dumb stones in the sky
but you slow down, you can only travel so far

You dwindle, and you cannot take credit
for space or fire

You haven't discovered

*

Time, all the time you have
is itself a ward of the void

*

Every evening some meaning passes over and marks
the door with a stain, sometimes of love, good will.

Most days focus on protect, preserve, maintain.

And the night comes.

You float off to sleep in the fetal position.
The folded seed of what if.

Picket fences

He decided some winter morning
to walk through the yards
and gardens of neighbors

kicking boards out of picket fences.
Riveted to the task we followed.

We loved the swing of boards
as they loosened, the nails kicked out
like teeth through wood.

I see by the light of what
we considered a brilliant idea

that we listened to what he wanted
to do, to create a secret passage.

Like water we broke through
and like animals nobody saw us that morning
and we ran over the frozen dirt of diamonds
to hop a fence with expert freedom.

And that one friend whose idea it was:

How long had he been in charge of us
and from where did he take the power
and why did it ring true?

There was a royal carriage of fate about
the way he walked from his house and down
the street, looking back at him.

He was the eldest of us, passionate, intense
and worse, the heir and subject of his father's
anger and hate, carrying pride and disdain
as weapons and protection.

Years later we longer knew him

or his wish to escape, to tear
the air open and spray a trail
of will and impulse.

The sky would be a crown for his blood
but the end came at night, and obscure.

Ten thousand cars passed us

Children, pulling ourselves
up and down on zippers
of paths made in high
grass on the slope
of the freeway
in light and
heat and
shadows

Part of the sunlight plowing the planet
and part of the frost and dew falling

Part of the tail of creation ourselves

In time unrecorded
and time preserved

And pushed along like clouds
we ran the slopes

In the ignition of storm colors
and slick ether of rainbow light

An open, beautiful secret

Ten thousands cars

A million cars passing us

The animal sparkle of mystery
in our eyes

On the highway

Shaking their heads at the wheel

The tracheal break in the hills

The marble of mountains appeared

The concrete slabs of merciless summer
and the cooler pines at the picnic table

The green isolate silence of farms
and the pitch black of love in the park

The red dirt of the flooded desert

They sank into heat and animal joy

All they ever did was approach and approach
and never arrived and never planned, an end.

To find her door, to follow her dream
he scratched his movements into hers
where they led, following, following.

They were not wired to the world then

They moved and crackled with impulse

There were many roads that might have led elsewhere
and relics and sites of deaths and saints and the Virgin

Death in the kind of wind that could choke them
and from which they huddled through the night

They achieved the road and the middle of nowhere
in the pan of a valley scanned by the sun each day

Somebody's son and somebody's daughter did not pray

and did not wonder how it was they found each other

They were for leaving

They were for wobbling in the heat of the highway

like the other machines in the sun, and all of it now

and both of them, then, like scratches and glyphs in
in the air and rain, the evening, dawn and memory

They were for dreams which even now
return as inaccurate, perfect descriptions
of love bending them like wood in water and
joining them beneath contortions of stars.

dirt road

Wolves are walking through the night
to the front of my house.

I cannot sleep and I dream like a child
of meeting the dead on a Halloween night:

Again I visit a dream
and a girl capable
of calming me

who frolicked in costume
and yelled out

"I want what I can't have;
I haven't changed one bit!"

Out of the mouths

Spirits come and go
unable to be certified

Gray and full of night
the wolves march along
a road in my dream.

And when I wake up in the middle of night

I also meet the little girl
who is lamb, and she was tiger
and
       I love her
       as she skips in the beautiful
       mild night of October
with that costume tail waving in the street lamp
behind her.

I lie like a deer with the wolves

side by side
and we breathe calmly.

I dream like a child
ready to sit on the lawn
in the dew in the lamps
of the homes

with the wolves
and the little lamb girl
I don't know.

*

I dream like a star
or a deer

The child
The wind

Our blood
our lips
are warm.

Return

Standing in the black slab of river
crawling his chest

Possessions having sunk to the bottom

He hauled the canoe back to the bank

*

She evacuates his life.
He sleeps it off for months.

*

Later he sat and watched the day decompose
into yellow and red, purple and gray and lastly
the green of the dark vanishing forest

The last recognizable vegetable matter
dissolving into black mush of night.

*

One morning he stands
and knows he will go

Find the self
as if out of longing
for a once beautiful lake

And there
he will look
straight down to the bottom
and there at the bottom is the mirror
image of an adult's dumb face or tired glare.

To stare into that clarity is to beware.

Beware the bruise that opens

into a wound behind the eyes.

Beware the pulse
twitching in that part of the wrist kicking
between bones, the simplest and truest and
meaningless, beats, meaning life, and return

Because there are times he hated it, or said so.

There are times a man
is only a stump intelligence.

*

Return to the loneliness that had been
successfully ignored.

A black day will decompose.

The rest of a life will come.

Some days my limp goes to my arm

Some days my limp goes to my arm
and it flares with a burning pain

Some days the world enters
my foot and destroys the muscles
and symmetry and some days

The fire recoils in the heart
and the ashes that spurt
are the days left to me in the sun.

And some days I rise to find
I remain lame although I am
the very power and glory of life
in every hour of life

Look at my lame beauty and say

You are no different
I am not unique

The broken street

The street is broken

the city and world

our bodies
of pieces
of years

but
think of a whole
that remains

an acrobatic embrace
of breath and sky.

The street is broken

It's this winter and our spines buried alive
in the feeble evenings
but

Think of a motion
or flight

A way to know
beyond the motionless prison

I mean the eyes
or else the soul

Follow me

but I am no leader

Follow my shadows

Follow the valley

Follow

The risk
of stepping into air

of my strange face

Follow

Seeking you

Seeking

but I am no leader

But if you do not jump
Or if you do not run
Or of you do not fly
Or if you do not
Climb

Then sit

Let us not think of it anymore

Smile and I will smile

I too have lived in my failure to speak.

Joseph Hamel was born and raised in Detroit, attended Edwin Denby High School and Wayne State University and later studied at theatre conservatories and studios in New York City. His poems appeared previously in the Portland Review, Litspeak, and currently in Barrow Street Journal. His play DEPEW, a modern adaptation of Molière's TARTUFFE, in rhymed couplets, was a 2019 semi-finalist for the National Playwrights Conference at the Eugene O'Neill Theatre Center.

www.ingramcontent.com/pod-product-compliance
Lightning Source LLC
Chambersburg PA
CBHW021204090426
42740CB00008B/1224